Read Write Inc.
Phonics

Green Level

Book 3

Tug, tug

Created by Ruth Miskin

Stories by Gill Munton

OXFORD
UNIVERSITY PRESS

How to use this book

Support your child as they follow each of the steps below.
There are notes in italics to guide you throughout the book.

Before reading each story, ask your child to read the Speed Sounds, in and out of order, and then the **Story Green Words** and the **Story Red Words**.

When reading the story:

1   Help your child to sound-blend each word (unless your child can already read the word without blending). Praise your child for their effort!

2   Re-read the story to your child and chat about what is happening. (There are questions on the page after each story to help you.)

3   Encourage your child to re-read the story again. Praise your child for reading the words more quickly.

4   Let your child colour in the stars on pages 13 and 23 as they complete the activities for each story.

Contents

Story 1: *Tug, tug*

Speed Sounds — 4

Story Green and Red Words — 5

Tug, tug — 6

Questions to talk about — 12

Star checklist — 13

Story 2: *The web*

Speed Sounds — 14

Story Green and Red Words — 15

The web — 16

Questions to talk about — 22

Star checklist — 23

Glossary — 24

Speed Sounds

Each box contains one sound. Sometimes one sound is represented by two letters (a digraph) or three letters (a trigraph). The digraphs and trigraphs used in this story are circled.

Consonants

Ask your child to say the sounds (not the letter names) in and out of order.

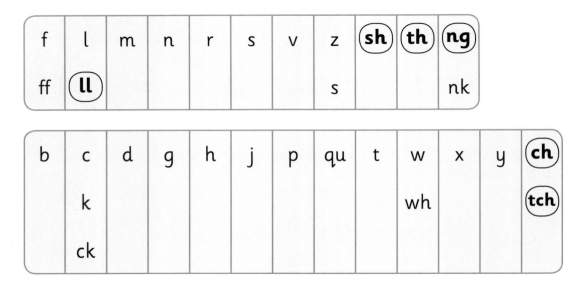

f	l	m	n	r	s	v	z	(sh)	(th)	(ng)
ff	(ll)						s			nk

b	c	d	g	h	j	p	qu	t	w	x	y	(ch)
	k								wh			(tch)
	ck											

Vowels

Ask your child to say the sounds in and out of order.

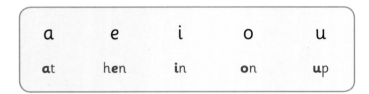

a	e	i	o	u
at	hen	in	on	up

Story 1 Tug, tug

Story Green Words

*For each word, ask your child to read the separate sounds (e.g. **g-o-t**) and then blend the sounds together to say the word (e.g. **got**). Sounds that are represented by more than one letter are underlined.*

got   his   rod   wi<u>ll</u>   ca<u>tch</u>   a   big

fat   and   yum   sat   <u>th</u>en   tug   yes

Ask your child to read the root word first and then the whole word with the ending.

fi<u>sh</u> → fi<u>sh</u>ing   <u>ch</u>ip → <u>ch</u>ips

Story Red Words

Red Words don't sound as they look. Read the words out to your child. Ask your child to practise reading the words.

I   he   said   no

Story 1
Tug, tug

Introduction

Black Hat Bob is fishing in his boat. He is looking forward to eating a lovely supper of fish and chips.

Black Hat Bob got his fishing rod.

"I will catch a big fat fish,"
he said.
"Fish and chips – yum!"

He sat . . .

and he sat . . .

No big fish.

Then . . . tug, tug.

"Yes . . . a fish!"
said Black Hat Bob.

tug tug

"Six bugs are stuck in my web," said Spin.

"A big black bug . . .

a bug with spots . . .

a flat pink bug . . .

a bug with six wings . . .

a fat red bug . . .

and a long thin bug."

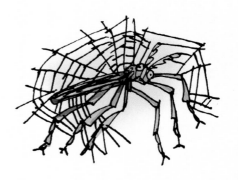

"I will get the six bugs and munch them up!"

But . . .

"I cannot stand up!"
said Spin.
"I am stuck in my web!"

Questions to talk about

Read the questions aloud to your child and ask them to find the answers on the relevant pages. Do not ask your child to read the questions – the words are harder than they can read at the moment.

Story 2: The web

★ What is the spider's name? (page 16)

★ How many bugs are stuck in his web? (page 17)

★ What does each bug look like? (pages 18–19)

★ Why does the spider want to get the bugs? (page 20)

★ What happens in the end? (page 21)

★ Have you ever seen a spider in its web?

Star checklist
Story

 2

I can read the Speed Sounds.

I can read the Green Words.

I can read the Red Words.

I can read the story.

I can answer the questions
about the story.

OXFORD
UNIVERSITY PRESS

Great Clarendon Street, Oxford, OX2 6DP, United Kingdom

Oxford University Press is a department of the University of Oxford. It furthers the University's objective of excellence in research, scholarship, and education by publishing worldwide. Oxford is a registered trade mark of Oxford University Press in the UK and in certain other countries

Series created by Ruth Miskin
Stories by Gill Munton
Illustrations by Tim Archbold

The moral rights of the author have been asserted

First published 2017

British Library Cataloguing in Publication Data
Data available

ISBN: 978-0-19-840814-7

10 9 8 7 6 5

Paper used in the production of this book is a natural, recyclable product made from wood grown in sustainable forests. The manufacturing process conforms to the environmental regulations of the country of origin.

Printed in Great Britain by Bell and Bain Ltd, Glasgow

Helping your child's learning with free eBooks, essential tips and fun activities
www.oxfordowl.co.uk

Glossary

Digraph a single sound that is represented by two letters, e.g. *sh*

Green Words words that your child will be able to read once they have learnt the Speed Sounds in that word

Red Words words that do not sound as they look, e.g. *the, said*

Root the part of the word that gives the most meaning

Speed Sounds the letters and the sounds that words are made up of (see pages 4 and 14)

Trigraph a single sound that is represented by three letters, e.g. *tch* in the word *match*